RED DEER

First published in Great Britain in 1999 by
Colin Baxter Photography Ltd
Grantown-on-Spey
Moray PH26 3NA
Scotland

Text © Tim Clutton-Brock 1999
Photographs © Neil McIntyre 1999

WorldLife Library Series

A CIP Catalogue record for this book is available from the British Library

ISBN 1-900455-57-9

Printed in Hong Kong

RED DEER

Tim Clutton-Brock

Photographs by

Neil McIntyre

Colin Baxter Photography, Grantown-on-Spey, Scotland

Contents

Introduction

Red deer are the largest and most striking land animal in Britain and there are few other wild animals whose history has been so closely intertwined with that of humans. From the first occupation of western Europe by man, red deer provided meat, skins and bone tools. Beautifully executed profiles of red deer stags occupy a prominent place in the Stone Age cave paintings of the Dordogne. After the end of the Ice Age, red deer became the single most important food species of many mesolithic communities and continued to be a major source of food, and of tools, after farming cultures spread throughout the continent. By classical times, human use of red deer had shifted from economic dependence to hunting for sport. The practice of hunting deer with hounds, or 'venery', continued and developed throughout the Middle Ages. It is still represented today in the West Country where deer are hunted with hounds (and eventually shot), as well as in several other European countries, including France and Belgium.

As the ancient forests were cleared from the face of Britain, red deer populations drew back to more remote and less hospitable areas. Today, England contains only four sizeable wild populations: around Exmoor in the West Country; in the New Forest in Hampshire; in Thetford Chase in Norfolk; and in parts of the Lake District. It is in the Highlands of Scotland that the largest and most significant part of the ancient herds remain. Here, over a quarter of a million red deer use the steep slopes and heather-dominated plateaux of the Scottish hills. Red deer are both a prominent feature of the wildlife of the hills and glens and a major source of employment and income in many of the remotest parts of the country. However, they are also a threat to the regeneration of many indigenous trees and shrubs, including heather and Scots pine. Controlling deer numbers and achieving a sensible balance between the interests of nature conservation, agriculture and sport is one of the major challenges facing land managers in the Highlands today.

Characteristics

Red deer belong to the Order Artiodactyla, which includes hoofed animals with even numbers of toes such as pigs and camels as well as sheep and antelope; to the Sub-order Ruminantia which includes the artiodactyls that digest vegetation by fermentation in a fore-stomach or rumen; and to the Family of deer, the Cervidae, which are characterised in most species by the presence of antlers in males. In some of the smaller deer species, like musk deer and Chinese water deer, males have large canines and no antlers, but in the larger species, including red deer, the canines have become small and non-functional and males carry large antlers, which are shed (cast) and re-grown each year.

Unlike the horns of sheep and cattle, antlers are true bone and develop from two outgrowths of the frontal bone, called pedicles. In red deer, young males grow their first antlers during their second year of life, shedding them before the beginning of their third year of life. Each year afterwards, they grow a progressively larger and more complete set of antlers until they are around seven years old, when the number of points stabilises, though the length may increase for a few more years. Once a stag is around 11 years old, his condition begins to deteriorate and, if he survives the winter, he is likely to start to 'go back', growing smaller antlers with fewer points.

In mature stags, antler shedding occurs in February and March, though it can be delayed by poor body condition. After the antler is shed, the bleeding cup heals over and immediately starts to grow a black stub of new bone, covered with a smooth layer of skin and short hair called velvet. Antler growth is almost complete by late summer, when rising levels of testosterone trigger the constriction of the blood vessels supplying the velvet, which rapidly shrivels and dies and is thrashed off in vegetation, leaving the antlers clean, and very sharp. Antlers are well designed as defensive and offensive weapons and a stag that has suffered a major breakage in one of his antlers is seldom able to fight effectively afterwards. Though the annual cycle of casting and re-growth involves energy loss in growing new antlers each year, it has the major advantage that it allows individuals that have broken their antlers to re-grow a new, unimpaired set the following year. In sheep and antelope, whose horns are not renewed each year, an animal that breaks a horn suffers a disadvantage for the rest of its life.

Female red deer (hinds) are smaller and around 35 per cent lighter than males. The larger size of male red deer has evolved because large size is important in allowing a stag to win access to a harem in the rut. Hinds do not need to compete, so there has not been such strong selection for large body size. In species of deer and antelope where a male defends a single female rather than a harem, there is not such intense competition between males for mating access to females and the sexes are generally of similar size.

Unlike other mammals, deer and other ruminants have no incisor teeth in their upper jaw and their lower incisors press against a callous or pad, allowing them to grip and rip off grass and leaves. Mouthfuls of vegetation are not chewed immediately but are swallowed down into the rumen where they soak in the animal's gastric juices, gradually softening as the result of bacterial fermentation. After a feeding bout is finished, the animal contracts its rumen, sending boluses of food back up to its mouth, which it repeatedly chews and re-swallows. Gradually, this process reduces the vegetation that it has eaten to small particles and these pass out of the rumen and down into the lower parts of its stomach and are digested.

Their sense of smell is well developed and, if you wish to approach red deer closely, it is best to move upwind towards them. Like other deer and antelope, they use olfactory signals to communicate and have well-developed glands in front of the eye (pre-orbital) as well as between the toes.

A typical hind group in summer, including (from the left)
a well-grown calf, two young hinds, the matriarch and a young stag.

Stags and hinds feeding on an exposed slope in spring. While red deer evolved in partially wooded habitats, they have adapted to the bare hills of the central and western Highlands. Here, they commonly form larger groups than in more wooded areas.

Distribution

Though they extend into the tropics, deer (Cervidae) have always been principally confined to temperate lands. Deer-like animals first became identifiable around 30 million years ago. By three million years ago, deer species very similar to red deer had colonised much of Europe and Asia, later spreading to North America via the Alaskan land-bridge. North American red deer (which, in America, are called 'wapiti') differ from European and Asian populations in their larger size, brighter rump patches and higher bugling call, and are sometimes classified as a separate species, *Cervus canadensis*. However, they are more commonly regarded as a subspecies of red deer and classified as *Cervus elaphus canadensis*. Wapiti-type red deer (*Cervus elaphus canadensis*) are not confined to North America and also occur throughout Asia north of the Gobi desert, overlapping with western red deer (*Cervus elaphus elaphus*) around the western end of the Tien Shan mountains. They are a very adaptable species and have been introduced to other parts of the world, including New Zealand where there is a large wild population as well as an extensive deer-farming industry.

There is one unfortunate quirk of nomenclature. In Europe, the large, browsing moose (*Alces alces*) are referred to as 'elk'. Perhaps because of the large size of the wapiti that they found in North America, the first colonists referred to wapiti as elk and the name stuck. As a result, when Americans refer to elk, they are usually talking about North American red deer (*Cervus elaphus canadensis*) while, when Europeans talk about elk, they are referring to moose (*Alces alces*).

Prehistoric red deer in Europe were very much larger than modern populations, though modern red deer in mainland Europe are substantially larger than Scottish deer and have relatively larger antlers. The small body size of Scottish deer is a result of stunting in the harsh and mineral-poor environment of the Highlands, for Scottish deer raised on deer farms reach weights and antler sizes comparable to those of European deer.

Red Deer in Scotland

The early history of red deer populations in Scotland was much the same as in England. As men gradually cleared the ancient forest, the red deer drew back to the remote areas of the Highlands and used high ground more and more. Before the development of accurate firearms, they were commonly hunted by driving them into enclosures. The Reverend Donald MacLean gives a detailed account of a deer drive on the island of Rum off the west coast of Scotland: 'On each side of a glen formed by two mountains, stone dykes were begun pretty high in the mountains and carried to the lower part of the valley, always drawing nearer, till within three or four feet of each other. From this narrow pass a circular space was enclosed by a stone wall, of a height sufficient to confine the deer; to this place they were pursued and destroyed.' The remains of one of these enclosures can still be seen on Rum.

Deer numbers declined during the eighteenth century after it was discovered that Blackface and Cheviot sheep could be kept on the upland pastures of the Highlands. The graziers quickly recognised the deer as a competitor to their flocks and, after 1750, deer numbers over much of the country fell further. By 1811, only six deer 'forests' (tracts of land devoted principally to hunting and not necessarily covered in trees) had large numbers of deer on their ground.

An unexpected development stopped the decline. Increased wealth, generated by the Industrial Revolution, led to a demand for shooting in the Highlands by English gentry. Developments in sporting guns and rifles made it relatively easy to approach and shoot red deer and a tradition of deer stalking sprang up, with its own practices, ethics and vocabulary, quite separate from the ancient tradition of hunting deer with hounds. By 1840, the number of deer

Deer will make extensive use of natural woodlands, and their browsing can halt regeneration.

forests had increased to 45 and attempts were made to control predators and poachers. Prince Albert's love of stalking, combined with the purchase of Balmoral by Queen Victoria in 1852, set the seal of royal approval on the sport and deer stalking entered its heyday. Gentry and wealthy English industrialists purchased estates, built roads, bridges and substantial shooting lodges. The area of ground covered by deer forests increased rapidly, from just under one million hectares in 1883 to nearly two million by 1912. A survey of the number of stags shot in deer forests immediately before the Second World War showed a total cull of around 10,000 stags and 8000 hinds. Deer numbers are thought to have declined between 1939 and 1945 as a result of increased shooting combined with poaching, though estimates of the extent of the decline vary widely, ranging from around 20 per cent to over 50 per cent.

After the war, public concern over organised poaching, as well as marauding by deer onto farmland, led to the establishment of legal 'close' seasons for stags (21 October to 30 June) and hinds (16 February to 20 October) as well as of an official body, the Red Deer Commission, whose duty was to further the conservation and control of red deer in Scotland. Forty years later, the Commission is still active, and has recently been renamed the Deer Commission for Scotland. Its members are selected by the Scottish Executive, following open applications and, in addition to the Chairman, include members nominated by conservation bodies and sporting, forestry, farming and landowning interests.

Between 1961 and 1970, the Red Deer Commission's stalkers covered around 80 per cent of deer ground in the Highlands and estimated that the total population of deer on open hill ground was about 185,000. Deer numbers rose to over 300,000 by the early 1980s, perhaps partly because many landowners reduced their sheep stocks over this period and partly because of a run of mild winters. There are thought to be somewhere around 250,000 to 300,000 red deer living on the open hill at the moment as well as sizeable populations living in the forestry plantations.

Stag groups form during the winter on low ground, in areas relatively little used by hinds. These groups often break up during the day and re-form in the evening. Members of the same group are clearly able to recognise each other and there is usually a well-defined dominance hierarchy among them, though this changes during the course of the antler cycle. Older stags are the first to cast and then become subordinate to younger animals – until these cast in their turn and the original order is re-established.

Grouping and Ranging

Visitors to the Highlands in summer often spend many days in deer country without seeing red deer. During the summer months, disturbance and biting insects drive the deer onto higher ground during the hours of daylight and you need to look up to the lower tops to see them. Once you have got your eye in, it is easy to distinguish groups of hinds from groups of stags. Hinds tend to be heavily bunched, each animal grazing close to several neighbours, while stags are more widely and evenly dispersed within the group. This difference reflects contrasting patterns of kinship: hinds generally associate with their mothers, daughters, sisters and their offspring and will tolerate their relatives grazing in close proximity. Stags leave their mother's range between their second and fourth years of life and move to join loose groups of stags in traditional wintering areas. Consequently, stags belonging to the same group are seldom closely related to each other and are less tolerant of each other's proximity than hinds.

Individual hinds have well-defined ranges, varying from around 0.5 sq miles (1 sq km) to more than 2 sq miles (5 sq km), which they seldom leave. A hind's daughters adopt ranges overlapping that of their mother, though they sometimes extend their ranges. Neighbouring hind groups have ranges which overlap and their members often form temporary parties consisting of hinds drawn from several groups. Neighbours seem to recognise each other, for hinds that are outside their normal range are frequently harried by resident animals.

Stags are less closely tied or 'hefted' to a particular area and individuals often have separate summer and winter ranges as well as separate rutting areas. After stags leave their mothers' groups they disperse more widely than hinds: studies show that while fewer than 10 per cent of hinds are shot over 5 miles (8 km) from their birth area, more than 40 per cent of stags are shot over 5 miles away.

In some parts of the Highlands, deer form large herds with others of the same sex.

Red Deer Year

The Rut

In the second half of the summer, stags gain weight rapidly. In July, their testes begin to grow, tripling in weight by early September. Levels of male hormone (testosterone) rise in their blood, first triggering antler cleaning and subsequently leading to the annual development of neck muscles and mane. In late September, stag groups fragment and individuals move to their separate rutting grounds in areas used by hinds. Records of individual stags show that young stags initially wander widely during the rut, while mature stags often return to the area where they first held a harem successfully. On the rutting grounds, stags join and herd together groups of hinds, defending their harems day and night from other stags. They roar repeatedly – a deep guttural bellow that echoes around the slopes and crags. Challenging stags roar repeatedly at their rivals, and competitors may exchange roars for 10 or 20 minutes. Stags use these exchanges to gauge whether it is worth fighting a rival for possession of his harem. Harem holders that roar more frequently than challengers usually beat them if there is a fight, and challengers seldom pursue their challenge if they have been out-roared. This may have substantial benefits to both parties, since the costs of fighting are high and individuals will increase their chances of survival by avoiding them. Roaring may also serve to attract and stimulate hinds: experiments show that hinds kept separately from stags conceive earlier if they are played tape-recordings of roaring stags.

When a challenger decides to press home his attack, he advances and the two stags often go into a parallel walk at right angles to the challenger's line of approach. Parallel walks can last for 10 or more minutes. At any moment, one

At the end of September, stags move to their traditional rutting grounds and start to establish territories, roaring repeatedly and marking the ground with urine.

stag may turn and lower his head, inviting his rival to do the same. The usual response is for both animals to drop their heads, run together, and lock antlers. When stags are fighting, the action is so fast that it is often hard to see precisely what is happening, but slowed-down film of fights shows that fighting stags use their antlers to lunge repeatedly through their opponent's guard as well as to lock and hold their opponent. Fights often last for up to five minutes or more, the two opponents corkscrewing round and round as each attempts to twist his rival into the downhill position. They are clearly dangerous: around 20 per cent of mature stags are temporarily injured each year and 5 per cent suffer a permanent injury. Temporary injuries commonly end the stag's rutting career for that year while permanent ones may do so for life. Studies of deer and antelope living in reserves where predators are common, show that predators selectively kill injured males so that, in the past, fighting probably had even heavier costs.

The fighting success of stags determines their mating success, since only stags that can defend harems successfully father many calves. In practice, a high proportion of calves are fathered by a relatively small number of stags: on Rum, fewer than 20 per cent of mature stags are responsible for fathering over 80 per cent of calves. Successful stags are usually of above-average size and weight, and their early development has an important effect; most stags that are successful fighters were well grown as yearlings and calves. It is often suggested that the relative antler size of stags reflects their fighting ability, and that antlers play a major role in displaying a stag's dominance rank. However, there is little evidence that this is so: stags with relatively large antlers for their size are not necessarily particularly successful fighters or breeders. The fact that stags that have broken their antlers are quickly beaten does not contradict this, for stags that have recently lost their antlers are seldom able to fight effectively.

Towards the end of September, the first hinds come into oestrus and the number of conceptions rises to a peak between the second and fourth weeks of October. Most hinds are in oestrus for 6 to 24 hours and, during this time,

Once they have cleaned in August or September, they return to using their antlers in threats and fights. Group members in hard horn commonly spar gently with each other (bottom), twisting their heads from side to side to explore the position of their points. After stags have cast their antlers in spring, disputes are settled in boxing matches. These contacts rarely develop into full fights, which are largely confined to the rut.

show intense interest in the stag, licking him and sometimes mounting him. It used to be thought that most mating occurred at night but, in practice, red deer mate throughout the day and night with peaks in the morning and evening. Stags usually mount a hind several times, eventually leaping clear of the ground as they ejaculate. Most hinds mate with a single stag in each rut and over 80 per cent of all conceptions occur in October, though a small number of hinds conceive in November and December.

Stags cease feeding almost entirely when they are holding harems and their condition declines during the course of the rut: successful animals may lose as much as 20 per cent of their body weight over this period. By the middle of October, the first stags are rutted out and begin to lose interest in their harems, drifting back to their winter ranges as smaller and younger stags take over their harems. Writing in 1576, George Turbervile provides a graphic description of the gradual change-over: 'Old harts [stags] go sooner to vault [mate] than the young and they are so fierce and proud that, until they have accomplished their lust, the young harts dare not come near them, for if they do, they beat them and drive them away. The young deer have a marvellous craft and malice for, when they perceive that the old harts are weary of the rut and weakened in force, they run upon them and either hurt or kill them, causing them to abandon the rut and then remain masters in their places.'

Survival

Hinds are pregnant through the winter months. By late February, they are at their lowest ebb and the outline of their backbones and pelvises can be clearly seen through their grey-brown winter coats, which have become sparse and pale. They move slowly and stiffly between feeding patches, spending as much

In bad weather, hinds and stags lie down, facing into the wind. Stags seem more sensitive to exposure than hinds and changes in weather have more effect on their distribution.

of their time in shelter as possible. Under extreme weather conditions, red deer feeding in exposed areas can lose twice as much body heat as they do in shelter, increasing their need for food and reducing the rate of digestion. They spend much of their time on low ground, sheltering behind outcrops or in woods (where they have access to them) and often straying onto farmland.

Deaths peak between late February and early April as animals exhaust their last reserves. The first to die are the weaker calves born the previous summer. In most Highland populations, around 20 per cent of calves that survive through their first month of life die in their first winter, though this may be as high as 35 or 40 per cent where population density is high and where the animals have reached the carrying capacity of their habitat. As in many other mammals where males are substantially larger than females, juvenile males are more likely to die when food is short than females. As a result, deer populations that are allowed to increase to a point where numbers are limited by starvation commonly show a strong bias towards hinds in the adult population. Next to die are older stags that used up their reserves during the rut and, finally, breeding hinds. In late winter, calves that have lost their mothers wander unhappily from group to group, getting kicked and threatened by unrelated hinds. Traditional belief had it that deer were very long-lived but even where predators and hunters are absent, few Highland deer live for more than 15 years. Most stags die between the ages of 9 and 12 while hinds live a year or two longer. Since few stags hold harems successfully before they are six or seven years old, and the fighting ability of most animals has started to decline by the time they are 10 or 11, their breeding careers are quite short. When a stalker reports that the same stag has rutted at the same site for 10 years, he will almost certainly have failed to recognise a changeover when the original stag was replaced by a younger contender.

In populations of red deer living on the open hill, hinds generally conceive for the first time in their third or fourth autumn although, in populations living in

In the central Highlands, the duration of winter snow cover exerts a strong influence on survival and condition. When snow cover is prolonged, mortality is high, and after cold winters calving rates are relatively low and coat change and antler casting are delayed.

woodlands or forestry, pregnant yearlings are not uncommon. Thereafter, hinds can conceive each year until they are 15 or more. Where animals are in poor condition, they often fail to conceive (or at least to bear a calf) in the year following a summer when they have reared a calf successfully and have suffered the full costs of lactation. These (temporarily) barren hinds are referred to as 'yeld' and their frequency in the population varies from less than 10 per cent, where deer numbers are low and food is abundant, to over 40 per cent where populations have reached the maximum the ground can support.

The fecundity of hinds normally starts to fall after they have passed their twelfth year, and the birth weight and survival of their calves drops at the same time. However, older mothers suckle their calves for longer and their offspring are often in better condition, and more likely to live through their first winter, than those of younger hinds. As a result, the production of surviving calves does not decline much with the mother's increasing age.

Feeding Behaviour

By April, the harsh climate of the Highlands is beginning to soften and the pale, faded stems of last year's grass are mixed with patches of brighter green as the hill grasses put out new shoots. The deer feed avidly at this time of year, trying to replace reserves lost during the winter months. Their appetite varies with the breeding cycle: even when stags are kept in the absence of hinds and have access to unlimited concentrates, their food intake falls between September and December and then rises to a peak between March and June.

Like other species of deer, red deer feed throughout the 24 hours. The 10 to 13 hours they spend feeding per day is divided into 6 to 10 bouts of grazing, usually lasting between one and two hours and interspersed with periods of rumination or resting. Grazing peaks in the evening during summer and winter

A group of stags and hinds. Outside the rut, such associations rarely last long.

with less time being spent grazing at night than through the day. However, where low ground is commonly disturbed by humans, there is a relative increase in night-time grazing.

Broad-leaved grasses, especially bents (*Agrostis*), narrow-leaved grasses, including fescues (*Festuca*) and heathers (mostly *Calluna vulgaris*) make up around 90 per cent of the deers' diet in most areas of the Highlands. In the eastern Highlands, heather is more abundant and provides a higher proportion of the diet than on the west coast, in some areas making up nearly 50 per cent of the animals' diet. In both areas, it is most heavily used in autumn and winter. Bilberry (*Vaccinium myrtillus*) is often used in the eastern Highlands and, in coastal areas, the deer will also eat seaweed (mainly *Laminaria* species) especially between November and February. Bones and cast antlers are chewed for the calcium that they contain, especially by stags.

Deer are highly selective feeders and only make use of a small proportion of the vegetation available to them. Many of the commonest grasses and sedges, including purple moor grass, bog cotton and deer sedge are little used by deer except during their earliest growth stages. In spring, the deer carefully select some patches of apparently similar vegetation more than others: research shows that they prefer areas where nitrogen levels are high. For example, in coastal areas, they show an especially strong preference for feeding on grassland around gull colonies where the grass has been enhanced by the droppings of the birds. Within particular feeding bouts, red deer usually move from one food to another, commonly eating a proportion of coarser forage in addition to the more nutritious grasses.

Stags and hinds differ in their use of habitat. In general, stags feed more than hinds in areas that offer a higher availability of forage but lower food quality, and they eat a lower proportion of narrow-leaved grasses and a higher proportion of heather, especially during the winter months. Nitrogen levels are lower in the food of stags and the size of the food particles in the rumen is larger, confirming

A two or three-year-old 'spiker' whose antlers have not yet started to fork. Antler size is strongly affected by early development. In most Highland populations, there are a few stags without antlers at all, which are referred to as 'hummels'. They usually constitute less than one per cent of adults. Until recently, it was thought that the loss of antlers might be under the direct control of genes (as is the absence of horns in cattle) and stalkers did their best to kill any hummels before they got a chance to breed. However, research suggests that hummels are usually animals that suffered a setback during early growth and never developed proper pedicles. By breeding from hummels taken from wild populations, scientists have shown that these deers' sons and grandsons grow normal antlers.

that they eat a coarser, less digestible diet. Differences in diet between the sexes are sometimes linked to differences in their use of high and low ground: stags commonly use higher ground than hinds in summer but lower in winter. The reason for these differences in habitat use is probably that hinds require a diet with higher levels of nitrogen to cover the costs of gestation and lactation, while stags need a larger amount of food on account of their larger body size.

Calving

By mid May, the pale hillsides of late winter have turned to bright green, interrupted by the darker colour of the heather stands. The deer have shed their bleached winter coats, and grown bright red-brown summer coats, with well-defined dark pointing around their rumps. Hinds are starting to show their pregnancy in their bulging flanks and rolling gait. Their gestation length of 33 weeks is at an end by early June and, one by one, they leave the main herd to give birth in pockets of sheltered ground on the middle or upper slopes of the glen sides. The first sign that a hind is about to calve is a swelling of the udder, usually one or two days before she gives birth. Hinds tend to give birth in the early morning or evening; calves are kept lying out in longer vegetation where they are visited two or three times a day by their mother. They select their lying sites with care, choosing long vegetation where they can see the slopes beneath them. Even where hinds are well used to humans, mothers become extremely wary, avoiding visiting their calf if a human is in sight and making skilful use of dead ground when approaching it.

The average birth weight of calves is around 14 lb (6.5 kg), although stag calves are born around 1 lb (0.5 kg) heavier than hind calves. Average birth weights vary considerably between years, ranging from 13 lb (6 kg) in cold years, when low temperatures have delayed the start of spring growth, to 15.5 lb (7 kg) in warm springs when grass growth is well advanced in May. Animals that are born light tend to remain (relatively) light throughout

Calves spend most of their first week of life lying hidden in long vegetation while their mothers graze within sight. Their lying places are carefully chosen and are usually raised above the surrounding ground and sheltered from sight on at least one side. They are visited every few hours by their mother who suckles them and then moves away to graze on her own.

their lives, giving birth to small calves in their turn.

Though approximately the same number of hind and stag calves are born overall, the proportion of male calves varies with food availability, as well as between different categories of mothers. After especially severe winters or when numbers are particularly high, a lower proportion of stag calves are born, probably because increased numbers of male foetuses die before birth and are resorbed or aborted. In addition, small, subordinate hinds tend to produce a preponderance of daughters while larger, more dominant mothers produce a preponderance of sons.

Mortality is high and around a fifth of all calves die in their first month of life. Golden eagles are common predators, quartering low over the ground in search of calves lying in the heather. If the mother is present, she will stand guard over the calf, protecting it from attack, but if she is feeding on low ground, the calf has little chance of escaping a determined attack. Young eagles are sometimes grossly over-optimistic in their assessment of what they can handle. Once, on Rum a young eagle was seen attacking a yearling deer, fastening its talons on its back and sending the animal careering down the hillside before the eagle was shaken loose.

Growth

By the time calves are two or three weeks old, their mothers return to their usual groups accompanied by their 'spider-legged' offspring. In mid summer, calves still in their spotted natal coats can often be seen chasing each other through the groups of hinds or exploring the sights and smells of their new world. Mothers continue to suckle their calves throughout the summer until they conceive again in October and their milk supply gradually dries up. If they fail to conceive, they will continue to allow their calf to suckle throughout the winter and into the following spring. It used to be thought that it was these yeld

Well-grown calves lying out with their mothers in August sunshine on the top of an outcrop.

hinds that produced the best calves since they are typically in very good condition by the following rut. However, research shows that their offspring are no larger or more likely to survive than those born to hinds that have reared calves in the previous years, probably because hinds which are unsuccessful breeders in one year are likely to suffer the same disadvantage in later years.

Calves grow rapidly throughout the summer, reaching a weight of around 55 to 65 lb (25 to 30 kg) by the beginning of winter. Stag calves grow faster

than hind calves, reflecting their larger adult size. As a result, their need for food is greater and they suckle more frequently from their mothers than hind calves. The costs of rearing sons are high: mothers that have raised sons successfully through the summer are more likely to die in the following winter and, if they survive, are less likely to breed the following year than mothers that have reared daughters.

As fresh grass becomes available the following April or May, calves begin to grow again but their growth slows or ceases at the onset of each successive winter. Hinds can

A golden eagle feeds on deer carrion.

continue to grow until their fifth or sixth year, stags until they are six or seven. In most areas of the Highlands, the average (live) weight of milk hinds lies between 140 and 170 lb (65 and 75 kg) while the live weights of stags average between 240 and 310 lb (110 and 140 kg).

Early growth rates have an important influence on breeding success as adults. Hinds born below average weight turn into small adults and, in their turn, produce light calves with a low chance of survival. Similarly, stag calves that are born light or are subjected to food shortage during their first winter are small as adults, and seldom get to hold large harems.

Stalker, client and ponyman (ghillie) bringing a stag off the hill. In many areas of Scotland, ponies represent the only feasible way of recovering deer carcases, though, in less rocky areas, tracked or wheeled vehicles are also used. Most estates operate a policy of selectively culling stags with small or poorly formed antlers, carefully selecting an individual stag before stalking it. Virtually all deer stalking is privately organised and controlled, in contrast to the U.S.A., where public hunting access is common.

Population Dynamics and Management

Red deer play an important role in the economy of the Highlands. Many of the larger estates still employ one or more stalkers whose job it is to guide the owner, his or her guests or shooting tenants on the hill, to decide which stags should be shot, to retrieve the carcase and to prepare it for sale. Where stalking is leased to tenants, the lease often specifies the areas of the estate that can be stalked and the number of stags that can be killed. The estate usually provides the services of the stalker and his ghillie or 'ponyman', who is responsible for retrieving carcases, but usually retains ownership of the venison. Hinds are culled in winter, usually by the stalker or by other estate staff. The total reported cull of red deer is currently around 65,000 animals per year, producing an annual income of 15 million pounds from stalking lets, as well as from the sale of venison and other deer parts.

Where deer populations are not culled by man and there are no natural predators, numbers will rise to a point where they are limited by food shortage. In Scottish populations that have reached this level, the average age at first conception is delayed, few milk hinds produce calves, growth rates are depressed and the mortality of calves and yearlings is relatively high. Adult mortality is less closely related to density and is high when harsh weather in autumn or winter reduces the availability of food. However, population density affects the influence of weather, and bad winters generate higher rates of mortality in populations that have reached carrying capacity, than in those maintained well below carrying capacity by regular culling. In conjunction, these changes slow the rate at which numbers increase until population size is stable.

Unfortunately, heavy grazing pressure by deer can have serious effects on their habitat, gradually destroying stands of heather and leading to the reduction or disappearance of herbs and grasses that cannot sustain heavy grazing. As deer readily eat growing seedlings, moderate densities of deer can prevent tree regeneration. Where nutrients are scarce and weather conditions are harsh the growth rate of seedlings is delayed, thus prolonging the period for which they are susceptible to being destroyed by browsing deer.

In many parts of the central Highlands, high deer densities have prevented the regeneration of the last remnants of the great forests of Scots pine that once dominated the lower slopes of the hills. Luckily, this can be reversed by reducing deer numbers. After purchasing Abernethy Estate on the edge of the Cairngorms, the Royal Society for the Protection of Birds (RSPB) found that few Scots pine were able to regenerate, and that the forest, and its associated bird populations, were dwindling in size. They swiftly reduced deer numbers to low levels, stimulating a rapid increase in regeneration of the pine forest, as well as in the numbers of many of the birds associated with it. However, in western Scotland, regeneration is harder to accomplish since the deer share their range with large numbers of sheep at densities far higher than deer. Though sheep eat a rather lower proportion of heather, they have much the same impact on shrubs and growing trees as deer, so that reducing deer numbers is unlikely to have much effect unless sheep stocks are also reduced.

Since the diets of sheep and deer overlap, the density of sheep affects the numbers, condition and breeding success of deer. Increasing sheep numbers generally leads to a reduction in the number of deer using the same ground, while the removal of sheep stocks leads to an increase in local deer numbers. Sheep may also influence the abundance of parasites shared by the two species (including liver fluke, lung worm, tapeworms and ticks) and may affect the incidence of common diseases (including leptospirosis, Avian TB and pneumonia).

The challenge facing land managers in the Highlands today is to reconcile the conflicting interests of estate owners, deer stalkers, shepherds, naturalists and hill walkers. In some areas, there may be benefits in reducing deer numbers to halt the erosion of heather and woodland. However, the ideal density of deer will vary with the aims of land management. Managers wishing to

maximise the numbers of sheep that their ground can support, or to encourage the regeneration of woodland, will wish to reduce deer numbers to low levels, while estates that depend on the revenue from stalking will need to maintain higher densities of deer. Fortunately, as a result of research on deer supported by the Nature Conservancy Council, Scottish Natural Heritage and the Natural Environment Research Council, there now is a much firmer understanding of the effects of different management policies, both on deer populations and on their habitat. New tools are available, including improved methods of counting deer, developed by the Deer Commission for Scotland, and a computer-based model (the Hill Deer Model) produced by the Macaulay Land Use Research Institute at Aberdeen, which uses measures of the area of different plant communities at different altitude levels to estimate the number of deer that the ground can support.

What the future holds is uncertain. Red deer have shown how flexible they can be by their initial invasion of the hills and glens, and should have little trouble in adapting to future changes in the management of the uplands. A more serious threat is the risk of hybridisation with Japanese sika deer (*Cervus nippon*), which have spread through the country in association with coniferous forestry plantations. Sika deer are now well established in south-western Scotland as well as in several areas of the Highlands and, where deer density is low, red deer and sika will interbreed, producing populations of hybrids that will readily breed with either parent species. Ultimately, as in parts of Ireland, local deer populations consist of a varied mixture of hybrids with few pure red or sika deer left. The island populations of the Hebrides which are protected by the sea against sika invasion are consequently an important resource for the future.

During the rut, challenging males test harem-holders by roaring
at them, using their response to assess their condition and fighting ability.

Distribution Map

Historical limit of populations of red deer and wapiti from Whitehead, 1972; Heptner, Nasimovich and Bannikov, 1988; Ward, Towell and Metz, 1982. In this figure, red deer and wapiti are classified as two separate species (*Cervus elaphus*) and (*Cervus canadensis*) though the two populations are classified as subspecies by some authorities. The precise location of the Asiatic boundary between the two groups is still uncertain.

 Cervus canadensis   Cervus elaphus

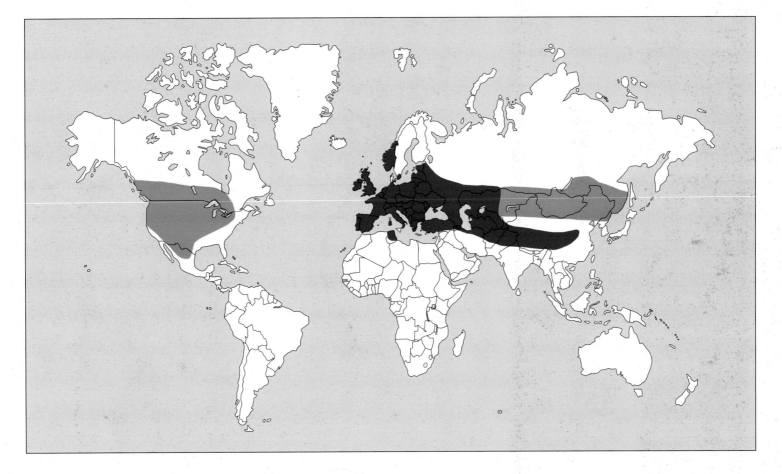

Reproductive Cycles of Scottish Red Deer

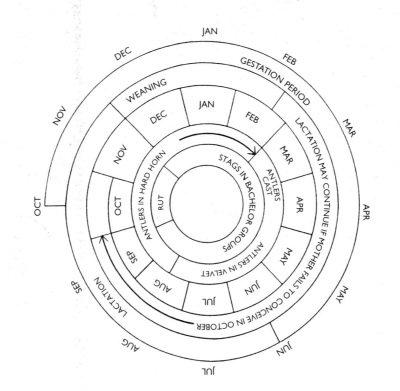

The outer two rings depict the cycle for hinds. The inner two rings relate to the cycle for stags. The mating season occurs in October, when more than 80 per cent of the hinds conceive. Calves are born in June and most are weaned 6 or 7 months later if the mother conceives again, but not until about 18 months after birth if the mother fails to conceive in the second autumn.

The outer ring of the cycle for stags shows the monthly state of the antlers. Mature stags cast their antlers in February and March and regrow new ones during the summer months. In August the velvet covering of the new antlers dies away and the stags enter 'hard horn', ready for the rut in October.

Red Deer Facts

Latin name		*Cervus elaphus*
Weight:	stags	230–320 lb (105–145 kg)
	milk hinds	154–220 lb (70–100 kg)
Usual age at first conception of hinds		15–40 months
Mating season		mid September to early November
Gestation		33 weeks
Calving season		mid May to early July
Age at adult weight	stags	6–7 years
	hinds	4–5 years
Number of foetuses		1
Birth weight		13.2–15.4 lb (6–7 kg)
Natural lifespan	stags	10–13 years
	hinds	12–15 years
Population density		1–>25 deer/km^2

(Figures shown are for Highland populations living on the open hill rather than in forestry plantations or deer farms)

Recommended Reading

There is a wealth of literature on red deer, ranging from scientific papers to J W Fortescue's unforgettable *The Story of a Red Deer*. For a readable introduction to the range of deer species, try G K Whitehead's *Deer of the World* (Constable, London, 1972); Duff Hart-Davis' *Monarchs of the Glen: a history of deer-stalking in the Scottish Highlands* provides a detailed account of the history of Scottish populations, while *Red Deer in the Highlands* (T H Clutton-Brock & S D Albon, Blackwell, 1989) offers a synthesis of what is known of the ecology and behaviour of Scottish deer. A J de Nahlik's *Deer Management: Improved Herds for Greater Profit* (David & Charles, 1974) gives guidelines for managers. Finally, there is a range of shorter publications of the British Deer Society (Fordingbridge, Hampshire SP6 1EF) including their quarterly journal *Deer*.

Biographical Note

Tim Clutton-Brock teaches animal ecology at the University of Cambridge and has led research on red deer on the Isle of Rum since 1972. He was the Chairman of the IUCN Deer Specialist Group and has published two books and more than fifty scientific papers on the ecology, behaviour and evolution of red deer.

Neil McIntyre is a professional photographer living in Strathspey in the Highlands of Scotland. His work has appeared in books, calendars, postcards and magazines, including *BBC Wildlife* and *The Field*. He has twice won the prestigious Eric Hosking *Wildlife Photographer of the Year* competition, as well as many other awards.